£1.99

43

D0480423

100 GREAT WATER-COLOUR TIPS

MIRANDA FELLOWS

CONSULTANT: HAZEL SOAN

B.T. Batsford Ltd · London

A QUARTO BOOK

First published in
Great Britain by
B. T. Batsford Ltd.
4 Fitzhardinge Street
London W1H 0AH

Reprinted 1995, 1996

ISBN 0-7134-7523-4

A catalogue record
for this book is
available from the
British Library.

This book was
designed and
produced by
Quarto Publishing plc
The Old Brewery
6 Blundell Street
London N7 9BH

Manufactured by
Bright Arts (Singapore) Pte Ltd
Printed in Singapore by
Star Standard Industries Pte Ltd

Contents

INTRODUCTION by Hazel Soan

THE SUN IS AT its zenith, the dazzling noon-day light creates short exciting shadows – your watercolour is looking good, but it's drying too fast ...

Painting the delightful debris of a picnic lunch, the crumbs of freshly baked French bread scattered over the chequered cloth – you want to erase your pencil lines and lighten the background, but you've left your putty eraser behind in the hotel room ...

If only you had a pocket-size book full of all those useful tips you know other people know but you don't, all your problems would be solved.

100 Great Watercolour Tips is a compilation of exactly those small gems of advice that make watercolour painting more manageable, more enjoyable and, dare I say it, easier!

Watercolour is an exciting and challenging medium. Beginners, in particular, can feel bewildered by a host of supposed rules. Even those artists like myself who paint regularly in watercolour and have acquired the confidence of practice find themselves locked into habits that would benefit from being broken. One word of advice from another artist can release a whole torrent of ideas. One seemingly simple tip can unleash a whole wave of creativity.

Sometimes you wonder just how an artist achieved a certain technique; you've searched through all the books on water-colour but still it eludes you. Maybe it was something so simple and basic that no-one bothered to mention it.

When I was asked to read the man-uscript of *100 Great Watercolour Tips* I was expecting to find that I already knew or had used most of the tips at one time or another. I was surprised and delighted to find a lot of ideas I'd never thought of, some of them so simple they seemed like common sense when I saw them in black and white. That is the beauty of the book: the majority of the ideas require no extra purchases, no extra space and no heavy reading.

The book is designed to make access to the tip you need as straightforward as possible. The sections are clearly headed, starting with a general section and then moving on to more specific areas. The 100 tips are divided into sections highlighting the most common problem areas for watercolour artists. They cover the materials used and the painting in progress, running through washes, special effects, highlighting and masking, with small sections on altering and erasing, body colour and coloured grounds, and brief tips on travelling light! This is not intended as a book on watercolour techniques. The tips are short and to the point and brightly illustrated in all but a few self-explanatory cases.

You can have fun just trying out some of the tips. A lot of confidence and new ideas result from playing with watercolour rather than trying to make finished paintings. This is true both for the beginner and for the seasoned artist. I have enjoyed experimenting with ideas in the Special Effects section, making quick tiny watercolours just to try out the effect. Some of these "dispensable" paintings have more vibrancy than a finished painting because they were done in such a relaxed and experimental manner.

100 Great Watercolour Tips is a book for "dipping into" as the need arises: perhaps before, definitely during, and undoubtedly after! It is the kind of reference book you need to keep with you and which can never outlive its usefulness. Its size makes it a practical addition to the art bag, paintbox or smock pocket.

I highly recommend this small volume. Don't leave it on the shelf; it is one of those books that is happier well-worn, paint-spattered and covered with thumb prints!

MANAGING YOUR WATERCOLOURS

One of the disadvantages of watercolour is that you don't always know what it is going to do. One colour has a way of running into another just when you don't want it to, and refusing to do so when you do. The tips in this chapter provide some useful hints on how to make the paint "behave itself", as well as giving practical basic advice on colours.

1 **PRESERVING PAINT** To prevent your watercolour pans from drying or cracking up, mix them with gum arabic. If you don't have any gum arabic, put a blob of honey or glycerine on to the dried-out pan instead. Allow the glycerine or honey to soak into the paint before you start using it. This will make the paint more soluble, while retaining some of the moisture in its composition.

2 **FASTER DRYING** If you are working in damp weather and find that your watercolour is not drying quickly enough, use a hairdryer to accelerate the process. However, be careful when working across very wet pools of colour, as the dryer can easily blow and smudge your work.

3 **ALCOHOL MEDIUM** If you do not have a hairdryer for speeding up slow-drying washes, try adding alcohol to your paint as an alternative. In the days before the invention of hairdryers, gin added to the paint water was a popular choice for accelerating the drying process as it evaporates more quickly than water.

4 **SLOWER DRYING** If you want to work over a long period with watercolour and so need to prevent it from drying out, mix it with ox-gall or a similar flow-medium which will retard the drying process. There are three ways of using flow-medium: you can prime your paper with it and then paint over it when dry; you can mix the medium with your water, and then use the water to mix your paint; or you can mix the flow-medium directly into the paint on your palette. An added advantage is that flow-medium increases the vibrancy of your watercolours.

5 **SOAKING THE PAPER** If you work slowly and watercolour seems to dry too fast for your requirements, soak the paper in water for at least 15–20 minutes before you stretch it and start painting. This will ensure that it stays wet for longer.

6 **THE BEST PAINT** Although it may seem expensive to buy artist's quality watercolours, they are worth the extra cost. Because there is a higher proportion of pigment to binder, the colours are purer and more intense. The paints are also available in a wider range of colours and many are more lightfast than their student's quality equivalents.

7 **WATER** Always have three pots of water at the ready when you paint: one of clean water for loading brushes and wetting the paper; one of constantly replaced clean water for mixing with the paint to produce clean, clear colours; and one for rinsing brushes while you work.

8 **WORKING BIG** When you work on a large scale, try mixing watercolours in containers, rather than in your paint box. This will enable you to paint quickly and smoothly without having to stop to mix more colours, and you will be able to store the fluid for following sessions, retaining the exact colour mix required.

9 **DECEPTIVE COLOUR** Do your watercolours always look washed out when you have finished? This may be because you used too little pigment with too much water. Very wet colour looks deceptively strong and will dry lighter.

The colours in this variegated wash are still wet, and appear bright and vibrant

Once dry they have paled considerably

10 **TESTING COLOUR** Always keep a small piece of watercolour paper beside you to test out the mixtures and strengths of colours before you use them on your painting. If you note down the colour mix by the side of each test mark, you will always be able to remix any colour for further applications.

Viridian + Cerulean

11

11 **KEEPING PAPER DAMP** If you want your paper to retain dampness throughout the painting process, place a cloth soaked in water underneath it and leave it there while you paint. To stop the paper from cockling, press it tightly over the cloth and attach the edges to the board with tape.

13 **WATER QUANTITIES** If you have trouble measuring out the right amount of water to mix with your watercolour, try adding the water to the paint with a pipette (a type of tube). This avoids overwatering or spilling water, and is also useful for sucking up paint from a palette and storing it in a bottle for later use.

12 **TESTING FOR DRYNESS** Touching the surface of your watercolour with your fingers to test how dry it is can easily leave grease marks on the paper, to which paint will not adhere. To test for dryness, try using the back of your hand instead. It is a more sensitive receptor than the fingers, and will quickly detect any remaining dampness.

14 **BETTER BLENDING** If you add a little gum arabic to your water when mixing paint, it becomes less runny and easier to blend. This is particularly useful if you are building up a painting in a series of small brushstrokes, as they will remain separate rather than flowing together.

In La Vere Hutchings' painting, "Monterey Bay", the sparkling effect of the breaking waves is created by reserving white paper

15 **REFLECTED LIGHT** If your watercolours look dull, you may not be taking full advantage of the whiteness of your paper. The brightness of watercolour paint comes from the reflection of light from the white paper back through the paint. Think of the paper as an extra colour on your palette, and let it do some of the work for you.

16 **DRIED-UP PAINT** Rather than throwing dried-out tubes of paint away, split them open and use the remains as pan watercolour. But be careful: some tube colours become less insoluble when dry, and will create a flaky solution, so test them out first.

17 **BLENDING TONES** To avoid harsh edges forming between light and dark tones, dampen the paper in both the light and dark areas to allow the paint to spread. Then lay the light tones down first, and allow the paint to flow into areas which will then be coloured with darker tones.

Elizabeth Apgar Smith, "Lilies" (detail)

18 **BACKRUNS** If you place wet paint next to an area which appears to be dry but isn't, the fresh watercolour will suddenly bloom into the semi-dry area, usually creating unplanned effects. This is called a backrun. To avoid them always check that areas you want to remain untouched are completely dry before adding fresh paint next to them. However, backruns can create interesting effects that enhance your work, and some artists exploit them deliberately.

In John Lidzey's lovely painting, backruns on the wall and window create attractive effects

WATERCOLOUR PAPERS

If you visit a specialist supplier you will find a bewildering variety of hand-made watercolour papers, but most artists use machine-made papers available from all art shops. This chapter will help you make an initial choice, and you can experiment with more exotic papers later if you wish. There are also tips on stretching paper and dealing with problems such as creasing.

AN ALL-ROUND PAPER Most watercolour paper is made by machine, though you can also buy handmade papers, which have a high rag content. These are expensive and not usually available in ordinary art shops. Machine-made papers come in different surfaces, of which there are three main categories: smooth (otherwise known as hot-pressed or HP for short); medium (sometimes called cold-pressed or CP but most commonly known as Not); and Rough (also cold-pressed but with a much more pronounced texture). Although some artists choose smooth or rough paper for special effects, the all-round favourite is Not, which has enough texture to hold the paint but not enough to interfere with colour and detail.

1 Handmade paper
2 Extra rough mould-made artist's board
3 Not paper.   4 Rough machine-made paper
5 Smooth machine-made paper.   6 Not paper

20 **HEAVY PAPER** If you want to experiment with textures and effects on watercolour paper, use a good, heavy paper or watercolour board which will take real punishment. A heavyweight paper or board will not need stretching and should soak up a lot of water without disintegrating. This helps to retain the transparent quality of the watercolour paint. You can also use a sponge to remove or add colour.

21 **STRETCHING PAPER** Thinner watercolour papers need to be stretched so that they don't buckle when paint is applied. When stretching paper, sponging the painting side can sometimes stir up the surface. To avoid this, smooth paper kitchen towel over a board. With the top side of the paper placed face down on the kitchen paper, sponge the back of the paper. The kitchen towel will absorb any residual water which has seeped through to the top side. Next, turn the paper over and remove the kitchen towel. Then tape down the paper with brown gumstrip. Using this method, the painting surface remains undisturbed, no dust or specks are picked up from the board, and any prior drawing remains intact.

Place the paper over kitchen towel

Lightly sponge the back of the paper

Secure paper to board with brown gumstrip

22 **REMOVING CREASES** If you have accidentally creased your paper while stretching or painting, it can often be smoothed out when dry by ironing the back of it with a warm iron. Lay it face down on clean white paper to protect the painting.

23 **BUCKLED PAPER** If your paper has buckled, it is often possible to stretch it after you have finished the painting, unless there is a heavy build-up of paint. However, be very gentle with the painted surface.

24 **FLATTENING PAPER** If your paper buckles, allow it to dry out completely, place it between two sheets of blotting paper and put weights over the top.

BRUSHES AND BRUSHSTROKES

Most people will know that the best brushes for watercolour work are sables, and that these are very expensive. But there are many other brushes you can use, such as household brushes which are ideal for large washes. This chapter will help you to make wise choices, as well as learn to exploit the marks of the brush so that they play a part in your work.

25 **LOOSENING UP** To loosen your painting style and add a sense of spontaneity to your painting, try holding the brush at the top end, so you are forced to make quick dashes of colour. This will prevent you from working too lightly.

Holding the brush at the top encourages a looser, freer approach and more expressive strokes

CHINESE BRUSHES

26 If you can only afford a few brushes, Chinese brushes are a wise choice. They can create both very broad and very fine marks, and large, round, Chinese brushes are not as expensive as the equivalent sable ones.

27 **TESTING BRUSHES** The better the quality of your brushes the better your brush marks are going to be, so check the quality of any round or pointed brush by painting a fine line with it. The point of a good brush should give a fine line whatever its size.

With a pointed brush the line created is delicate

With a rounded brush the line created is equally clean

BRUSH QUALITY A good brush should have a certain resilience. You can test for the spring of your brush by wetting it to a point and dragging it lightly over your thumbnail. It should not droop but spring back.

WATER RETENTION To test whether a brush will hold a suitable amount of water, try moistening it with your mouth. Do not try this with a paint-loaded brush, however, as trace elements from the paint can be retained in the body.

STRAIGHT LINES Although long, straight lines can be made using a round brush, for variety try a "writer" or a "striper", which were traditionally used for this role. Writers are long-haired sables which taper to a point. They are also called riggers, as they were used to paint the rigging on ships. Stripers are long-haired sables which form a chisel edge. Different size brushes produce different line thicknesses.

BROAD LINES

31 One-stroke brushes, commonly made from synthetic or ox hair, are good for creating broad lines. Short flats and long flats can also be used. They are all chisel-edged and held in flat ferrules. Short flats are particularly suitable for applying short dabs of colour, while long flats hold enough paint for you to make one stroke across your paper.

DIFFERENT BRUSHES

32 Remember that the larger the brush head, the more paint it will hold, so make sure you have a range of brush sizes for different applications.

WASHES

The first skill the watercolourist must master is that of laying a perfect flat wash. This takes a little practice. However, as this chapter demonstrates, there are many ways of ensuring success, and you can then move on to more ambitious projects, such as graduated and variegated washes and working wet into wet.

DAMPENING THE PAPER For a really even flat wash, dampen the paper with a sponge or large brush to help each "band" of colour to flow into the adjacent one.

SPREADING COLOUR If the paint "furs" downwards (spreads in little, feathery lines) when you are painting a wash on wet paper, tilt the board sideways or diagonally to disperse the colour in all directions.

35 **ALTERNATIVE WASH BRUSHES** An old, worn-down shaving brush or a decorator's brush are both very effective for creating really large washes.

37 **EVEN TONE** If a flat wash is uneven in tone, you may not be charging your brush fully enough. Do not press too hard with your brush, and do not overcharge it with paint or you will create unwanted streaks. Once you have laid down a wash, avoid going over it again as this will definitely result in streaking.

36 **FLAT WASHES** When painting flat washes (washes that are the same colour and tone all over), always mix more paint than you think you will need. The wash will be spoiled if you have to stop and mix more paint.

GRADUATED WASHES When creating a wash that blends from dark to light in the same colour, lay the first band at full strength, and then dip your brush first into the water and then into the paint for each successive band. This ensures that the wash mixture becomes lighter by the same amount.

Robert Tilling makes expressive use of washes in "Grauville Bay, Jersey"

UPSIDE-DOWN WASH If a graduated wash needs to appear more concentrated in colour towards the bottom of the paper, turn the board upside down and start from what will be the bottom, working towards the top.

MERGING TONES When you have completed a graduated wash, work over it gently with a clean, damp, one-stroke brush to merge the change in tones.

VARIEGATED WASHES To create successful variegated washes (ones in which different colours are blended), apply each colour side by side, and let them bleed into each other.

Yellow applied next to wet blue

Where the two washes merge they create a third colour, green

MUDDY COLOURS If you often achieve muddy results with variegated washes, you could be working too fast, with the result that the colours bleed into each other too much. To avoid this, apply your first colour, then let it start to dry before adding the next. Use only one stroke of the brush to apply each line of wash. Work methodically in this way until you have applied all of the washes. Judging when to add the next colour is a question of practice and experience.

In Alan Oliver's "Poppy Field", the colours are fresh and clear

43 **DROPPED-IN COLOUR** If you want to add special effects, like light-coloured clouds, try dropping clear water into semi-dry paint. To create more dense effects, drop Chinese white or white gouache on to a damp wash. A very liquid, darker colour will bleed into the surrounding wash and produce more dramatic effects. Experimental washes such as these, might form an attractive background for a still life, suggest clouds, storms or distant trees, or provide an abstract quality.

Water is dropped onto still-damp blue paint

Adding Chinese white creates more dense effects

The colours merge to create abstract patterns

A darker liquid colour creates dramatic effects

44 **MEETING AN EDGE** If you only want your wash to cover part of the paper – for example, when painting a sky round chimney pots – start laying the wash from the edge of the chimney pots, rather than having to meet this intricate edge when finishing the wash. Tip the wash away from the pots' edges to prevent pools of paint gathering there unless desired.

45 **MASKING OUT** If you do not seem able to create clean washes over areas that you have blocked out with masking fluid, try to create the colour density and effect you desire with only one stroke. If you work over the wash with further strokes the effect will be less successful.

46 **IMPROVED COVERAGE** If white pinpricks appear on the surface of your watercolour paper when you are painting a wash, mixing a drop of ox gall into the paint will both increase its flow and help its coverage.

47 **PENCIL WASHES** You may have problems in creating broad washes if you use watercolour pencils. One method, on pre-wetted paper, is to scrape dry pigment with a scalpel from the pencil point on to the wet paper. Brush this in to dissolve the scrapings. Alternatively, scrape pigment into a dish of water until the desired density of colour is reached and then brush it on to the paper as if it were watercolour paint.

Scrape the pencil pigment on to wet paper with a scalpel

Brush the scrapings into the wet paper until they dissolve

48 **SOAKING UP DRIPS** If you find that drips collect at the bottom of your paper when you are painting a wash, place soft tissue paper across the area where the wash is intended to finish, and it will soak up all the drips.

EXCESS WATER To avoid leaving a thick pool of paint at the bottom of the paper, pick up the paint from the previous stroke as you work your way down the paper, mopping up the edge of the paint as you progress. When you reach the bottom of the paper, carefully pick up the pool of colour which has accumulated there with a just-damped brush.

 WET-IN-WET If you always seem to be left with pools of water when you are creating wet-in-wet washes (painting into an area that is still wet), you might be applying the second layer of paint before you have allowed the paper to soak up enough of the first wash. As water soaks into paper, it begins to lose its shine. Once a lot of the water has been soaked up, a brushload of paint will still flow freely, but you will have more control over it. When the paper loses its shine completely, but is not yet dry, you can control the paint you apply even more, while still being able to achieve soft-edged effects for such subjects as bushes or trees against a horizon.

51 **RETOUCHING** If you try to retouch a semi-dry wash you will be left with blotches. Let it dry completely first, then dampen around the area and touch in gaps with the point of a brush.

52 **REMOVING A WASH** If a wash is developing in patches, stripes, backruns or with any other unwanted effect, flood the paper with water immediately, lay blotting paper over the area and lift it all out. Repeat if necessary. If part of the wash has already dried, wait until it is completely dry, then brush clean water over the entire area. The paint should then spread out evenly.

The wash is first flooded with water

Blotting paper is pressed onto the wet paint and then removed lifting the colour away

SPECIAL EFFECTS

One of the joys of painting is discovering what the medium can do, and through the decades, watercolour painters have invented and perfected many different methods and "tricks of the trade". Some of these derive from exploiting the "happy accidents" that occur in watercolour work, for example a wash that has gone wrong and formed blotches and runs can suggest a whole new approach. With practice you will find your own watercolour tricks and techniques, but why not benefit from the experience of others initially, and try out some of the fascinating methods shown in this chapter?

53 **SOFT GLAZE** To create a soft glaze over dry work and to vary the surface colours, use a diffuser to blow out a fine spray. For the best results, make sure that the watercolour is completely dry before you add the spray. You can use a mouth diffuser – sold for applying fixative in pastel work – or experiment using a plant spray, which is also useful for redampening watercolour paper while you are working. Do not hold the diffuser too close to the work while spraying, or you will make areas of the paint run into pools.

A quantity of paint is mixed and applied with a plant spray

This creates an uneven "wash", adding surface texture

PAINT RUNS If you want to create an unusual wash while the work is still damp, direct a soft spray of water on to the surface. It will dislodge the damp pigment, causing it to run into surrounding areas. If the area sprayed is very wet, most of the colour will run. If it is fairly dry, only a little will run, leaving a light coloration in its path. Once you have sprayed the surface, you can direct the water's run by guiding it with a brush or by tipping the painting slightly. Alternatively, allow the paint to run freely. Using this technique, you can blend one colour into the background or bring a background colour into the foreground. Spraying an area of more than one colour will produce a more interesting run than a single colour.

INK BLOTS You can use watercolour inks experimentally to free up your technique and also as a novel way of suggesting the texture of foliage, flowers or pebbles. If you drop ink from a height it will form a blot. You can produce different effects by changing the height, diluting the ink, tilting the paper, flicking the wet ink to form spatters or blowing on the wet ink so it makes tendrils. Sometimes the random effects formed will suggest a subject that can be developed more representationally, at other times the effects will simply make a pleasing background.

SOFTENED EDGES If soft features such as clouds look too strong against a wash, use a cotton bud to blend the edges into the wash while the paint is still wet.

Ink dropped from a height blots and spatters

Blowing on wet ink creates tendrils

Experiment with different random effects

EXPERIMENTAL TEXTURES Don't be afraid to experiment with texture. Try applying paint with a variety of domestic tools, including potatoes, card, rags, razor blades, sandpaper, rubber spatulas and credit cards. Rub or scratch them over the paper.

57

Rubbing into paint with sandpaper

Spreading paint with a piece of card

PENCIL TRICKS To create interesting textures with watercolour pencil, take two different-coloured pencils and scrape pigment off them. Then wet a large round brush and pick up traces of the pigment scrapings. Paint directly on to the paper or the watercolour to create unusual blends and textures.

SPATTERING Rather than following the normal practice of using a toothbrush for spattering, flick a pre-wetted brush across the tip of a pencil. A moist, thin brush will give a fine effect, while a large, very wet brush will give a more generous, random result. This effect can be achieved on wet or dry paper.

Large wet brush with wet paper

SPECKLED EFFECT To add interesting texture to your work, try scraping dry pigment from a watercolour pencil over wet work. As the pigment flakes, it will stick to wet areas in the painting. You can then blow any excess away when the paint has dried.

BLOWN TEXTURE Allow a variegated wash to dry completely then blow paint down a straw, following the line of the paper upwards to create interesting textural effects.

SPONGING A small, natural sponge dipped in a pool of watercolour and dabbed on to the paper will create interesting effects for such features as foliage, rocks or sand.

63 **GRAINY TEXTURE** To create a texture similar to sand or snowflakes, try sprinkling grains of coarse salt into wet paint and then brushing them off once it is dry.

La Vere Hutchings has used salt spatter in her painting "After the Frost", of which a detail is shown here

64 **ROLLED-ON COLOUR** To apply a textured wash of colour, squeeze some colour from a tube on to a piece of glass or plastic, then mix it with a small amount of water and apply it with a roller on unevenly dampened paper. The roller will disperse the colour in blotches over the driest areas of the work, creating interesting textures. In the more heavily dampened areas, the paint will spread evenly on to the paper, leaving soft edges.

65 **ADDING SHINE** A brushful of gum arabic mixed with the paint makes it slightly shiny and more viscous. It allows the paint to dry on the surface of the paper instead of sinking in. This makes lifting off the paint very easy. Interesting wet-in-wet and textural effects can be achieved with this slightly slower-moving paint, especially if you splatter it with water or another colour when dry or half-dry. A drop of gum arabic mixed with strong colours will prevent them from looking dull and flat – any more than a drop will cause the paint to go shiny, and it may crack in time.

66 **MIXED MEDIA** Watercolour washed over wax crayon, pastel or oil pastel creates exciting textures and has the added advantage of binding the medium underneath.

67 **LIFTING OFF** Blot out un-wanted runs, bleeds or blocks with highly textured kitchen paper. This is particularly effective on medium-surfaced (Not) paper. It will not leave a smooth mark, as blotting paper does, but the imprint of the rough surface of the paper.

68 **USING MASKING FLUID** If your painting is dry and a particular colour is too strong and needs lightening, try using masking fluid as an alternative to blotting paper or a damp sponge. Apply the fluid over the area to be lightened, allow it to dry, then remove it.

Masking fluid has been used to create a soft, broken highlight

SPECIAL EFFECTS

UNDER THE TAP

Unusual effects can be achieved by running hot or cold water over your painting at various stages of its development.

Flowers are painted strongly

Cold water poured on paper

Paint spreads, blurring lines

More paint is applied

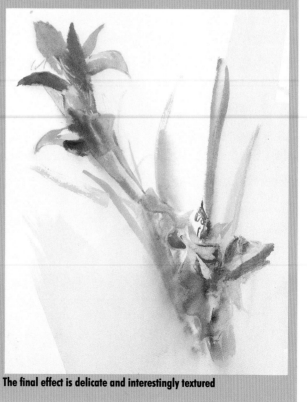

The final effect is delicate and interestingly textured

WASHING OFF If you are using a heavy or pre-stretched watercolour paper, you can create a texture effect by laying washes, allowing them to dry and then washing them off. Place your work at a slight angle, then wash the pigment away carefully with a hose. The harder the spray, the more pigment it will remove. Any very thin applications of watercolour will have been almost totally absorbed by the paper's surface and very little of the colour will wash away. Heavily painted areas, however, can be cleanly washed away and may leave an interesting texture. Remember that staining pigments, like alizarin crimson and viridian, leave more colour behind. Sedimentary pigments, like cerulean blue and Naples yellow, tend to sit on top of the paper and lift off more cleanly.

HIGHLIGHTS AND MASKING

Because watercolours are transparent, white highlights are achieved by reserving, or painting around the shapes to leave bare paper. Aids such as masking fluid make this once-tricky process much easier. And even if a highlight has become "lost" there are many ways of saving the situation.

 LIGHTENED HIGHLIGHTS Once your painting is completely dry, you can emphasize highlights by rubbing over them gently with a typewriter eraser, sharpened to a point to increase accuracy. This removes some of the top layers of paint, occasionally rubbing down the surface of the paper, and enhances the brightness of shafts of light. The nature of the eraser makes it easier to enhance very specific details.

 WIPED HIGHLIGHTS While a wash is still wet, use a piece of cotton rag to wipe out highlight lines. If the wash has dried, use a dampened tissue to do the same. This technique is particularly effective for light clouds or shafts of sunlight.

SCRATCHED HIGHLIGHTS Use a scalpel to scratch out colour to create detailed highlights. Ensure that the watercolour is completely dry before doing this – not just touch-dry.

ERASER SUBSTITUTE If you use an eraser too vigorously, it may break up the texture of both the paper and the paint. Crumbs of bread make a gentler eraser to clean up highlights. Knead the bread until soft and then use it in the same way as you would a conventional eraser. Do not apply too much pressure or the bread will crumble.

HIGHLIGHTS AND MASKING

LIFTED HIGH-LIGHTS
To create highlights while a wash is drying, use a dry brush to lift the colour out of the area. You will need to repeat this several times because the colour will continue to seep into the highlighted areas until the wash is nearly dry.

GILDED HIGHLIGHTS An unusual way to pick out highlights in a watercolour painting is to apply gold leaf to areas to be lightened. This is an effect which the painter Samuel Palmer often employed.

First apply size and allow to dry for 20-25 minutes

Use kitchen towel to apply gold leaf on the areas you wish to highlight

After two to four hours brush excess leaf away. Burnish

PASTEL HIGH-LIGHTS
If a lost highlight cannot be regained by any standard method, soft, pale pastel tints used over the area and lightly rubbed in will retrieve the highlight.

MASKING WITH PAPER To create random white areas, mask the paper with torn pieces of newspaper before applying your initial washes. For quite crisp effects, do not remove the newspaper until the wash is dry.

Washes applied over random pieces of paper

The paper is removed, leaving white shapes

Final touches of paint complete the work

79 MASKING FLUID HIGH-LIGHTS

A series of small highlights can be difficult to achieve by reserving white areas of paper. It is far easier and more effective to paint the required shapes with masking fluid.

Doreen Bartlett, "Poppy Field"

REMOVING MASKING FLUID If you find it difficult to remove masking fluid cleanly, you may be leaving it on the paper for too long. Once dry, the fluid should be removed as quickly as possible. The prevailing temperature and humidity will affect its drying time. It may help to keep a ball of used fluid, like an eraser, and when you are ready to rub your masking fluid off, roll the ball across it, always starting at the edge. Rolling is also less likely to tear the paper.

ALTERNATIVE MASKING FLUID A good alternative to using masking fluid is Copydex glue, mixed with an equal amount of water and a little non-staining pigment so that you can see where you have placed it. Non-staining pigment will also help you to see masking fluid.

PROTECTING BRUSHES To avoid ruining your brush when using it to apply masking fluid, work very quickly and clean your brush out as soon as you have finished. You can protect your brush by lathering some soap and coating the bristles with it before dipping the brush into the masking fluid. This will not affect your application of the fluid, and will also make it much easier to remove once you have finished.

83 **BRUSH SUBSTITUTES** Instead of applying masking fluid with a brush, try using a pen for masking out fine lines, and cottonwool buds for larger areas.

84 **CANDLE WAX** Wax from an ordinary household candle can be used instead of masking fluid to "block" the paint. It is, however, more difficult to remove than masking fluid, and is thus usually left on the paper to provide an interesting texture.

Washes are laid over masking fluid applied with a cotton bud

This has produced very even, regular white shapes

Washes applied over masking fluid applied with a pen

This produces much finer lines than can be made with a brush

Hot candle wax has been dripped onto the paper before the paint is applied

ALTERING AND ERASING

Watercolour painting can be a nerve-racking business, as things often go wrong. But you seldom need to throw the paper away and start again if a wash dries blotchy or if you find you have slopped paint over an edge that was meant to be white. There are many ways of making corrections, and if you are dissatisfied with a finished picture why not draw on top of the paint with coloured pencil or pastel?

BRUSHING OUT If you think that the edge of a brush-stroke is too hard or soft, and you want to achieve smooth edges, tickle them out with the tip of a damp brush.

REMOVING PAINT Trying to move watercolour once it has dried can be difficult, but it is possible. Once your watercolour has dried it can still be re-wet, moved around, or partially removed from the paper. A sponge may work better than a brush for this purpose. Bear in mind, however, that most colours can never be completely removed because the pigment in the paint will have stained fibres in the paper. Let the paper dry thoroughly before repainting.

87 **DISGUISING STAINS** After washing out a wrong tone or colour, you may have been left with a slight stain. You can paint a thin film of white or suitably tinted acrylic over this, smoothing the edges with a cottonwool bud. When the acrylic has dried, transparent watercolour can be washed over it.

White acrylic masks mistake   **Cotton bud blends white**   **Watercolour is re-applied**

88 **ACRYLIC SEALER** If your watercolour paper is too absorbent, or has become roughened by too much rubbing, a thin wash of white or tinted acrylic will seal the surface. When using acrylic for underpainting, or corrections, it should be used thinly, otherwise superimposed layers of watercolour may not adhere.

89 **CRAYON REMEDY** Coloured pencil or pastel on top of an abandoned or aborted watercolour can pull it all together, and create attractive effects at the same time.

In Hazel Soan's "Fish River Canyon", coloured pencil gives texture

OPACITY

Watercolour is usually thought of as a transparent medium, but it need not be. Some of the great watercolour painters of the past mixed their colours with opaque white paint, and many contemporary artists follow the same practice. If you want to give the paint more body, there are substances you can add to it, such as soap or starchy water – and you won't even need to visit the art shop for these.

TINTED GROUNDS Try tinting watercolour paper with diluted coffee. This was a common practice among early watercolourists, and is still a very good way of producing a pale, warm ground. In China, artists use tea-leaves to produce similar grounds. You could even tint paper with a used teabag.

ORDER OF WORKING You do not have to follow the convention of painting from light to dark with watercolour – Turner certainly did not always adhere to this practice. Working on blue-tinted paper, he would first apply "body colour" (opaque watercolour), building from dark to light as in oil painting, the reverse of the traditional watercolour process.

Diluted white paint modifies the darker colours

OPAQUE MEDIUM To make your brushstrokes more opaque, follow Turner's example and mix your paint with rice water. You can also try soap, which thickens the paint nicely and leaves small bubbles if applied with a stiff brush.

 OPAQUE PAINT Mixing gouache with Chinese white or white gouache will produce more opaque pale colours. You could also try undiluted watercolour, for example, yellow ochre, or cadmium yellow, on coloured Ingres or Canson papers.

with water

undiluted

with gouache

Thicker white paint is now used

White mixes with colours to create a milky effect

49

TRAVELLING LIGHT

It's always a problem going to paint in an unfamiliar place because you may encounter quite unexpected different colours. But resist the temptation to buy a whole new set of paints – take as few as possible and welcome the opportunity to practise your colour-mixing skills. Some of the greatest watercolours of all time were painted with no more than five or six colours.

94 **ADVANCE PREPARATION** If you like to work on tinted paper, prepare it in advance, so that when you arrive at your chosen location, you will be ready to get painting. You could even prepare several sheets, mixing up a large quantity of the desired colour.

95 **RESTRICTED PALETTE** If you use tube paints, and are uncertain which you will need, take only two versions of each primary colour – red, yellow and blue. This will give you valuable practice in colour mixing, and will also help to unify your paintings. Experiment at home before you go.

96 **RANGE OF TONES** When painting out of doors, you may not be able to take a wide palette. If you experiment, you will find that with one colour you can create infinite tonal variations – for instance, raw umber can appear as everything from a dark brown to a brick brown to a yellow ochre to a cream, simply by the addition of more water.

97 **COLOUR PATCHES** Choose the colours you will need from a set of watercolour pencils, and rub a 5cm (2in) square of dry pigment from each on to the last page of your sketchbook. Take this, a brush and some water and, when you are ready to paint, just wet the brush and touch it to the squares of colour. You can then blend them and paint on the front pages.

98

WATER SUBSTITUTE If you run out of water, or need to mix colour on a palette without much water, a touch of saliva makes an adequate alternative to water.

99

FINGERNAIL TRICK When painting on location without your usual "tool kit", use your fingernails if you need to scratch out dry paint for highlights.

100 **ALTERNATIVE ERASER** If you find you have left your eraser behind, dry French bread left over from your picnic can make an excellent alternative.

LANDSCAPE

When painting landscape don't make the common mistake of becoming bogged down in detail – think about the painting as a personal interpretation of nature, not as a copy of it.

KEY ELEMENTS It is all too easy to become bogged down in the detail of a landscape rather than see the work as a whole, so that your picture becomes too busy and your final image does not hold together. To create a convincing landscape, concentrate on a few interesting features and use creative licence. To practise this, half close your eyes to blur the image in front of you, and reduce it in your mind's eye to basic areas of tone and form. By freeing yourself of detail, you will find it easier to concentrate on those elements which will make your landscape more successful.

UNIFIED COLOUR Paint the sky first and then allow the tonal values across the land to complement the air mass above. To unite the colours in your landscape, repeat sky colours in the landscape below, using blues among the greens, for example. To create a sense of depth, use cooler colours towards the mid-distance and warmer ones in the foreground.

CLOUDS To gauge the true colour of white clouds, hold a piece of white paper against the sky and note what tonal variations there are. You may be surprised to realize that few are really white. When the light of the sun is shining directly through a cloud from behind, the outline of the cloud will be clearly defined. If there is no direct sunlight through a cloud formation, the outline will be much more hazy.

CONVINCING REFLECTIONS To test the effectiveness of your reflections, turn your painting upside down and see how convincing the image seems the "right way" up.

UNDERWATER SUBJECTS When painting subjects submerged under water try to make the surface waterline as clear as possible to ensure that the water retains a sense of depth. To create a fine edge, sharpen a suitably coloured watercolour pencil to a point and lightly mark in the line with it.

Subject is painted

A light wash of sky colour is brushed over the reflections

REFLECTED COLOUR The colours of reflections in water should both mirror the colours of the reflected object while incorporating the main colour affecting the surface of the water – usually that of the sky. To achieve this balance, try painting a light wash over the reflection using the same colour you have used for the sky.

The colours of the reflections are slightly richer than those of the buildings

The waterline is marked in

The line has helped to create a sense of depth

TREES AND FOLIAGE

The main cause of failure when painting trees is poor observation; look for the real colours of foliage, trunks and branches instead of painting everything in shades of green and brown. Texture is important too.

TRUE COLOUR If your trees look unconvincing, you may have allowed preconceived ideas about their true colour to stand in the way of a realistic depiction. Tree trunks are not usually brown – they are often, in fact, a mixture of greys and greens, and are similar in tone to their branches and leaves.

When painting trees, try to integrate the colours of the bark with those of the leaves

TONES AND ANGLES Do your trees appear flat? If so, make sure the branches protrude at different angles and directions to one another. Include tonal variation through the trunk, branches and leaves by diluting your colour as you work towards the branches and twigs. As the tree branches out, so the colours will become paler.

Donald Pass, "Commemorative Monument to the Queen's Visit"

TREE HIGHLIGHTS
Highlights give form and substance to a tree, and enhance the textured nature of the bark.

Alan Oliver, "Woodland Clearing"

FOLIAGE The texture of foliage can be hard to recreate in watercolour. A good way to achieve convincing texture is by using wax crayon or oil pastel over flat, dry watercolour.

A household brush is ideal for large blocks of colour

Wax crayon or oil pastel can be added once colour is dry

The mixture of media creates interesting textured effects

DRY BRUSH TECHNIQUE To create textured foliage, dip a brush into the paint, then fan out the bristles between your thumb and forefinger, pressing the bristles on to the paper while you paint.

Roy Winstanley, "Estuary, Dorset"

FRESH FLOWERS To convey the organic nature of flowers, paint the overall shapes in lightly, then try dropping in the centres of the flowers wet-in-wet, re-wetting any flowers that have dried with clean water. Allow the paper to dry off, and then fill in the fine details either with a brush or watercolour pencil. In this way, your flowers will appear as a vivid combination of spontaneity and intricate design.

Overall shapes blocked in lightly

Centres painted wet into wet; watercolour pencil details

LEAF PATTERNS To create a pattern of leaves or foliage, try applying paint with a sponge, dabbing first a lighter tone of say, yellow, then laying a darker tone of green or orange over the top to create the shadowy areas.

Sponging dark colours over light gives depth

LEAF VEINS Once you have applied the initial wash of colour to the petals and leaves of flowers, mask out the veins while you build up tonal variations. When you have finished, remove the masking fluid; the delicate veining will give the leaves and petals greater authenticity.

Masking fluid is applied over dry wash

Tones and colours are built up with further washes, and the fluid is removed

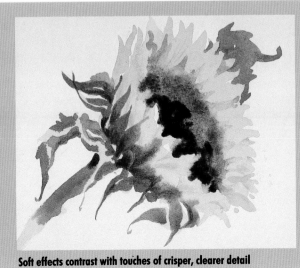

Soft effects contrast with touches of crisper, clearer detail

BUILDINGS

Watercolour is well suited to painting buildings, as the combination of broad washes and fine, delicate brushwork can describe architectural features with accuracy and sensitivity.

BRICKWORK When painting a brick wall, remember that from a distance not every brick will be clearly defined – rather the viewer will see the overall fabric of the wall, so describing a few bricks here and there will suffice. Begin by laying in a pale wash of raw sienna to provide the background tone. When dry, use a No. 6 chisel brush to paint the bricks and leave spaces between them to indicate mortar. Bricks are not uniform in colour, so mix three or four tones before you begin and alternate between them. When the first washes are dry, paint a weak solution of Payne's grey over the top of the brickwork to unify it. Finally, spatter a mix of Payne's grey and raw umber over the surface to create more pronounced textural effects.

The bricks are painted with a chisel brush, leaving white spaces for the mortar

SHADING STEPS To paint steps, apply a thin line of paint under the ridges of the steps, and, using a wet brush, pull the paint downwards to form the shadow, blotting out rogue runs which you do not want shaded. Alternatively, try wetting under the ridge of the step with plain water first, and then, while it is still wet, draw a line of colour under the ridge, allowing it to run into the clean water. Make sure that the band of clear water covers the whole of the vertical plane of the step, but is not so wet that the colour runs right down it.

WARM TONES Burnt sienna, with its rich, luminous red tone, makes a good colour for adding warmth to natural brickwork.

STRAIGHT STROKES To avoid crooked window frames, use the brushruling technique: hold a ruler at the correct angle to the paper and then carefully draw the brush along it with the ferrule held tightly against the edge of the ruler.

Three or four tones are used to enhance the texture

A light spatter of Payne's grey builds up the texture

The loose series of brushmarks creates a convincing impression

A thin line of paint is applied under the ridges of the steps

A wet brush is used to soften the edge

Alternatively, draw a line of colour under ridge

PAINTING PEOPLE

Although portrait painting is best avoided until you are sure of your skills, painting people in landscape is no harder than painting trees or rocks, and will often give the painting that extra touch it needs.

SKIN TONES If you find it difficult to achieve lively skin tones, try using smooth (hot-pressed) paper instead of standard cold-pressed. Because it has a much harder, flatter surface it will not soak up watercolour so quickly, making it easier to move the colours around and create soft effects. If you decide to experiment with this surface, you will have to control more backruns and pools of paint. Although the paper is more unpredictable, it will enable you to achieve spontaneous and sparkling results.

PEOPLE IN A LANDSCAPE It is best to paint them in with two simple strokes, one lighter to indicate flesh tones and the other over the top when dry to indicate hair or headcovering and garments. The overall shape of the stroke is important: it must be simple and direct.

Light brushstrokes over dried washes suggest the figures

Darker colours are now added for hair and clothing

The figures are well integrated into their surroundings

LAYERED TONES Build up skin tones gradually, with very thin, light washes of paint, allowing the painting to dry in between applications to achieve subtle tonal variations. The less you drag the paint around, the more lively the portrait will be.

La Vere Hutchings' "A Day at the Beach" is a perfect example of layered tones (detail)

FLESH HIGHLIGHTS When painting pale skin, allow untouched white paper to depict the lightest flesh tones.

In Paul Bartlett's "Face Looking Through", the colours have been worked rapidly wet into wet

ACKNOWLEDGMENTS

The author would like to acknowledge the invaluable hints and tips given by the following artists and experts while researching this book: Rosalind Cuthbert, Jean Canter, Moira Clinch, Charles Glover, Hazel Harrison, Emma Pearce (Technical Adviser, Winsor & Newton), Hazel Soan.

Quarto would like to thank Sally Launder, Debra Manifold, Hazel Soan and Mark Topham for demonstrating the techniques.

Quarto would also like to thank Daler-Rowney and Langford & Hill for supplying paints and equipment.

Art editor Clare Baggaley
Designer Clive Hayball
Photographers Paul Forrester, Chas Wilder, Laura Wickenden
Picture researcher Laura Bangert
Senior editor Sally MacEachern
Editors Diana Craig, Hazel Harrison
Editorial director Sophie Collins
Art director Moira Clinch

Typeset by Poole Typesetting (Wessex) Ltd, Bournemouth
Manufactured by Bright Arts (Singapore) Pte. Ltd
Printed in Singapore by Star Standard Industries Pte. Ltd